ALMOST LOVED

-- Poems --

Rena Joy

2024

Almost Loved copyright © 2024 by Rena Joy.

All rights reserved. No part of this book may be used or reproduced in any manner whatsoever without written permission except in the case of brief quotations embodied in critical articles and reviews.

For more poetry
TikTok @renajoypoetry
Instagram @renajoypoetry
www.renajoypoetry.com

Cover and internal design by Amy Smith Publishing.
Author Photo by Coral Konanz Photography.
Edited by Shelby Leigh.

Published by Amy Smith Publishing.

ALMOST LOVED

Trade Paperback: 978-1-0690381-0-4
EPUB: 978-1-0690381-1-1

Published in Canada
Printed in Canada / United States of America

1. POETRY / Women Authors 2. POETRY/ General

10 9 8 7 6 5 4 3 2 1

To all the girls who should've been loved from the start.

Preface

May 14th at three pm was the last time
I felt my mother's arms around me.
The last time I saw her smile at me.
The last time I heard her voice.

Then poof.
She was no longer permitted
to be my mother.

Eight years later, I was allowed a photo.
The only photo I have of my mother and me.
For years my mother didn't exist.
For years a little girl wondered,
what she had done
to suddenly become unloved.

Trigger Warnings

Abuse.
Violence.
Attempted Suicide.

Take care, dear reader.
Seek support.
You're never alone.

Contents

The Unlovable Girl	1
Murky Middle	19
Dark Nights	51
Out of the Fog	67
BIG Love	95
The Lovable Girl	117

"What if you spend
the rest of your life chasing love,
only to find her cowering
in the pit of your stomach?

What then?"

The Unlovable Girl

Meet the Unlovable Girl

The unlovable girl
wasn't born unloved.
She was created
during the many lonely nights
wasted, wailing on top of her
four-drawer dresser.

She should've been asleep,
tucked safely in her bed,
dreaming of a life worth living.

Instead, she filled her heart
with unshed stories—
convinced, if she remained small,
she could earn her new family's love.

Loved Once

I was loved once, I think.
By a mother who lost me
(although the beat of her resides inside me).
By a father unknown (???).
By a foster mom who was sick.
By half siblings I don't know
(do they think of me?).
By a brother who died
(when it should've been me).
By friends who come and go
(mostly go).
By my second parents who don't get me
(did they ever try?).
By a god who taught me love and fear
go hand in hand.
By a family who will read this
(will they?).
By a woman
wishing she could trust love.

Are You Ready to Know Me?

I can whisper a name
that I don't know.
I can give you a place
that has never been my home.
I can you tell a story, many in fact—
in colour, or shades of grey.
Most likely I won't.
My stories (unloved, outsider, scapegoat),
I'm not sure
you're ready to hold.

Please be ready.

My Name Mattered

I don't think about my birth name often,
although names are supposed to have power.
Maybe that's how I lost my magic—
it slipped away, waiting to be reclaimed.
The before me feels too foreign to embrace.

Stripped

I had a birth name.
It was scribbled on the back of a drawing,
tucked beside a rare photo of me.

Then I was renamed
like a dog from the pound—out of time,
taken, but never chosen.

How confused I must have been;
how confused I still am
that before me wasn't enough.

The Little Things

I acknowledge my dogs
with pets and chitchat and treats and toys
and whatever else pet lovers do.
I wish I could swap places,
for even a second,
to know what it's like to be that loved.

What I Wish the Kept Understood

I lost:
my mother,
my father,
my brother,
my sister,
my ancestors,
my history,
my name.

I'm not allowed to grieve;
grieving is for *real* trauma.

God gave me saviours.
Celebrate!
I'm happy!!
That's what's commanded of me!!!

Historical Grief

I grieve for the girl
who doesn't know her firsts.

(History matters.)

A Question I Keep Asking

Who am I
in a world that demands perfection?
I'm pitied, weighed down
with untold stories
wishing to be asked:
Will you t*ell me your story?*
Your truth doesn't scare me.

Make Yourself At Home

I'm trying to be real.
To let you into my labyrinth,
so that maybe
you'll get so lost,
you'll have to stay.
I can finally get some rest,
knowing tomorrow, you'll still be here.

Pluviophile

I'm a rain girl
living for storms,
a moment
I'm not expected to shine.

Tomorrow,
I'll play in puddles,
be a child renewed
to live again in the sun.

Life Unspoken

Sometimes, I listen to the same track
over and over and over.
The entire ride home
I bellow, I whisper,
I nod in silence.
Each beat shifts with my mood
as I search for comfort in words I know.
I'm soothed by a voice I wish I had.

Kept Vs. Unkept

Kept children aren't the same
as unkept children.
One knows themselves;
the other searches.

(I'm still searching ...)

A Grounded Life

Could I be the girl
who lives amongst the flowers,
breathing the wild air,
letting nature sing to me?

Could I welcome back the bees,
taste the sweetness
of spring beginning?

Could I let the summer heat
linger in my bones,
coated in a flowery perfume?

Could I watch the wildflowers bloom,
knowing soon
they will wither and die?

Could I be at ease,
grounded,
taking the seasons
as they arrive?

Could I just be?

I. Someone Worthy of Love?

~~Me?~~

   You.

~~Me?~~

   You.

~~Me?~~

   You.

~~Me?~~

   You.

~~Me?~~

   You.

~~Me?~~

         You.
       Always You!

Murky Middle

Broken Heart

I've never had my heart broken
from the boys I've dated.

My heart was already shattered
by the man who was supposed to
love me the most.

growing up small

the problem with growing up small
is it doesn't prepare you
for hips widening
to match fatty breasts.

suddenly, you're wearing stolen clothes
that don't fit right.
shifting and chafing,
they leave a trail
 of sludge-filled memories.

growing up small
is holding weight bones can't bear.
osteoporosis before even a single grey hair.
adulting in a brain
that doesn't know how to fire.
decades spent on couches and in gyms
stretching to fit a cracked mold.

growing up small
reappears with a flinch,
tainting hugs
and good-morning playfulness.

growing up small
is a battle of falsehoods,
a test of self-love.
if you're lucky,
a rewiring to stand straight.

Rage Monster

Memories are magical
like bedroom forts
and midnight drives.

Memories are sharp
like the butcher knife
you chased him with.

Memories are salty
like bear hugs and shoulder rides
after a basketball game.

Memories are pin pricks,
him slammed against
a door of nails.

Memories are juicy,
like watermelon drips
and belly laughs.

Memories are holes
punched through drywall,
patched but weakened.

Memories are safe
curled up beside you,
chasing away bad dreams.

Memories are double edged,
the brother I loved
and the monster within.

Dissociate

I zone out,
not because I don't care.
I want to hear about your day,
but sometimes I'm caught
between memories so crisp
my body retreats before I snap.

I try to be present
to cheer you on.
I care. I promise I love you,
but sometimes
the voices are too busy
praying for a better version of me.

Awake Just Barely

Sometimes when I'm napping,
my phone buzzes.
There are never new messages—
just me daydreaming that someone
cares enough to think of me.

There are no real friends
when you are too scared to reach out.
No one likes the chained dog
that has learned to bite.

I slip back to a place
where I'm loved
and wanted
and thought about
outside of holidays and birthdays—
even then I'm easily forgettable.

People Pleaser

I'm stuck in a tar pit
weighted with your expectations.
I'm fuel for your latest gossip,
useful to everyone
but me.

I'm Lonely

I can't tell you what happened.
I can't reveal the hurt me.
My words won't come.
My stories are lost, punched down deep,
treading acid in the pit of my stomach.
I'll stick to the fringes of movies and jokes.
Our encounters are void of deep truths.

Can't this moment just be happy?
A pause before I crack?
A break before I drown?

I'm flooded with grief
you can't possibly hold.

Cabbage Patch Doll

Adoptees are great pretenders.
We play house to be kept.
Drowning our grief
in gratitude, we serve you.

We center your feelings,
while our hearts long
to find the pieces of us
sealed and forgotten.

We are survivalists,
pretending our bodies
don't remember our mother's voices,
or our father's touch.

We are your children now.
We belong to you
like that plastic dollhouse
in the backyard.

You're the better life,
so we'll keep on playing
with our Cabbage Patch dolls—
anything less is disloyal.

Loneliness Probably Killed the Cat

Have you ever felt so alone
that if your cat died
instead of reaching out
to your scroll of friends
or hundreds of followers
or your workplace "family"
or even your lover
you opt for a sleepless night
on the couch
and a puffy-eyed morning
and another long day
of swapping shallow stories
as you choke back tears
that will leave you breathless
and wailing on the drive home
to your lonely house
with a cat to bury?

Maybe I'm Not a Good Person

It's been a heavy week.
A future-shattering,
sleep-until-noon,
nap-until-dinner week.
News ripped through hearts.
A reminder that karma's a bitch
with a case of mistaken identity.

Different // Not Better

Adoption
isn't a synonym for a better life.

What It Means to Be Abandoned

I had two fathers—
one I never knew,
one I wish I never met.
I don't know what's worse—
never having fatherly love,
or losing the love I should've had.

Breakfast at Denny's

Little trauma or big trauma
I can't tell anymore,
is holding back our worst day
while my family parades in front of me
a get together they all had weeks to plan.
Still, they question why I can't come
with no notice.

"You're being disloyal."
(I'm crumbling inside.)

"You're choosing your husband over us."
(He is my family; he is my safety.)

Still, my mind works on a solution.
(Maybe my boss will insist
I use vacation time I have yet to earn.)

Something on my face makes my father smile.
I grow quiet and fill with sludge,
waiting for the safety of my car to ugly cry.

My husband holds me,
telling me I can go
even though it would mean
abandoning us
on our worst day.

11/12

Love Odds

Two fathers.
Two chances at love.
What are the odds
they both wouldn't love me?

(The odds weren't in my favour.)

Blood Doesn't Matter Until It Does

Isn't love supposed to be a birthright?
Maybe that's why I'm so damn hard to love.
Your DNA doesn't run in my veins.

Thanksgiving

I had to work,
during the last family supper
before your death.
You stopped by the shop
with a plate and a hug
and an I love you.
I know it's true.

When I see pictures from that day
of the joy I missed—
it's a reminder that I wasn't family,
except to you.

Ho, Ho, Ho!

I hate Christmas—
the not being heard.
(The TV is on.)
The triggering of shame.
(I can't afford presents.)
The made to be small.
(I'm not worth the bus fare.)
All the shoulds,
lingering in my bones.
(Be perfect. Remain small.)

I hate Christmas
for all the things
it should've been
but never was,
spoiled by your hatred of me.

The Men In Our Stories

In my home
things were never explained,
so I hid in closets
and made believe I was Cinderella,
carrying a role
my brothers were never assigned.

In my home
women didn't feel
while their worlds imploded,
yet the men in our stories
weren't always wicked.
Sometimes there were epic battles,
all-night games,
and untainted love.

They could be charming—
the Jekyll and Hyde
of our fairytale.

I could be loved and unloved
in the span of a page turn,
searching for a happy ending
I wasn't yet old enough
to create,
begging to be protected
by a mother
who didn't dare leave.

The Silence is Echoing

Shut up!
You talk too much
about everything and nothing.

Shut up!
I've had enough
of random facts and useless chatter.

Shut up!
My program is on.
You're nothing but a bother.

Shut up!
Do as you're told.
Girls should be seen, not heard.

Shut up!
You're being annoying.
Wanting attention isn't a need.

Shut up!
Shut up!
Shut up!

Behind the Mask

If I disappear,
will you think of me:
the quiet girl,
the broken girl,
the lazy girl,
the never-smiles girl?

If I'm these things to you,
then I'm already gone.

Did You Know?

Did you know how to mother—
to hold me, to care for me,
to love me?

Did you feel my kicks,
fast or slow?
Did you feel anything at all?

Did you hear my cries,
babbling joy?
Did you hear yourself
louder than my wails?

Did you know what the papers meant—
to withdraw your care
forever?

Did you see a better future,
childless and alone?
Did you see the social workers coming
to sever our connection?

Did you know I would break
not knowing you?
Not knowing parts of me?

Either way, I forgive you.

(The system expected you to fail.)

Ogress

It's a myth first mothers
don't love their children
A retelling
to put them in their place.

Mothers Unknown

I don't know my mothers—
the mom I lived with, the mom I lost.
I don't know what's worse:
not remembering who birthed me,
or not knowing who raised me.

You're Just An Angry Adoptee

When I tell you my story,
instead of holding my hand,
you fill my space with exceptions—
taken from all the adoptees
you seem to know—
without being willing to know me.

Train Wreck

I've been on this night train for a while.
Chug-a-lug-lug. Chug-a-lug-lug.
I close my eyes and dream of derailment.

The conductor calls, "All aboard."
Buckle up. It's going to be a long ride.

1st stop: Loserville.
2nd stop: Nasty Girl.
3rd stop: Shame and Blame.
4th stop: Burn it All Down.
5th stop: Merry-Go-Round.
6th stop: Do the World a Favour ...
7th stop: You Still Here?

The conductor calls, "Last stop."
There is no getting off, not tonight.

Liar, Liar, Pants on Fire

I lied on my intake form.
I never tried,
never contemplated,
blissful silence.

One, two, three.
Sip. Pop. Sip. Pop.

Screaming but silent.
Desperate but hopeful.
Unraveling into an eternal hell.
The hell you say I'll go to
if I'm successful.
The joke is on you—
I'm already burning.

Four, five, six.
Sip. Pop. Sip. Pop.

I'm too much, but never enough.

I'm drowning,
        drowning,
                drowning.
Reaching, reaching, reaching.
Gasping, gasping, gasping.
Living but dying.
Not today,
unsuccessful.

Extinguished

I lied on my intake form.
I didn't want the record
of my inadequacy, my selfishness.

I lied on my intake form
to avoid the labels
(broken, unattached, ruined).
I'm not these things.
I'm not my trauma.

I lied on my intake form.
I was ready for help, yet not.
It was so long ago—
does it matter?
I didn't succeed; no second attempt.

My record has been corrected.

The What Ifs

I'm fine, more than fine.
I'm energetic.
Positively nostalgic
for a life that could've been.

There is no going back.
I wouldn't survive
a second trip.

Build Me an Arc So I May Grieve

We don't talk about you—
how the world was better
with you around.
How you filled me up
to survive another day.

We don't talk about you,
like not remembering hurts less.
You slipping away
cuts deeper
than stories ever could.

Year after year,
you're washed away
by unwitnessed tears
in fear we weren't made
to survive the flood.

But I'm still standing,
missing a brother
I want to share with the world—
an imperfect being
worthy of remembering.

Would I Be Happy as a Flat Earther?

If the world was flat (it isn't),
I would make all my shoulds
walk to the end of the earth
and drop off into nothingness,
leaving me to rest,
instead of playing shoulds on repeat
like a scratched record:
I should (get up) ... *do better.*
I should (go out) ... *try harder.*
I should (be happy) ... *just smile.*
I should become a Flat Earther.

Complex PTSD

I don't want to crawl back
to moments that wreck me.
That make my rage unbearable.
That bruise my insides,
leaving no trace.
But I see the mistrust
in my hesitations,
my sorrys,
my withdrawals from joy.

To you, I'm an asshole
when I'm trying to survive.

Wish Upon a Star

I want to love myself
like the morning raising the sun.
My essence always shining,
despite overcast skies,
despite eclipses,
and wars with the moon.
The world can't survive without me.

Looking for Love in All the Toxic Places

I didn't go looking for love
but you found me,
long past niceties
and pumpkin coaches
and godmother promises.

I thought I should love you
after all this time.
But then I hurt you on purpose.
Tit for tat.

Still, I tried to keep you believing
we could last forever,
when it was my turn to pay.

To Be Continued

He loves me … (I'm smart!)
He loves me not (I'm broken.)
He loves me … (I'm beautiful!)
He loves me not (I'm damaged.)
He loves me … (I'm witty!)
He loves me …

(Please don't stop loving me!)

Life On the Ledge

I'm comfortable here
on the ledge,
catastrophizing everything
that is good,
playing peek-a-boo
with a life I want.
There is no way to stop
this game that doesn't involve
                              jumping,
and a painted sidewalk
of insides no one asked to see.

I'm comfortable here,
dreaming of escape,
running away from   joy.

I'm comfortable here,
but you won't let me stay
in moments that wreck me.

You help me reframe all the ways
my brain leads me astray ...

Always pulling me
from thinking,
              thinking,
                            thinking,
and into feeling
the heartbeat of thriving.
Your patient love
calls back forgotten grit
to scrape bone and blood off dirt.

Love Through It All

The hardest part about loving someone
is when they can't see their own light.
Or, how their presence lingers,
guiding you through darkness,
lifting the world from your chest.
You know you couldn't have walked
through hell without them,
or recognized your beautiful self
in the mirror.

You say you love them.
You show them.
You remind them.
Bit by bit,
they believe you
like they believed in you.

Out of the Fog

Things I'll Never Understand

You built hearts
while destroying mine.
You inspired dreams
while stomping on mine.
You changed lives
while almost ending mine.
You loved your sons
while hating me.
I'll never understand.
As a mother now,
I can't forgive you.

We Don't Walk to Be Trendy

We like to blame the child for walking away
when the parent held all the power.

We like to scrutinize:
He loved her. (No, he didn't.)
He helped her. (For a price.)
He did the best he could. (Except change.)

We like to ask for proof,
to judge who's right.

We like to minimize:
It wasn't that bad.
He was nice to me.
You must forgive.

We wonder why she didn't say anything.
She screamed her pain a thousand times
until her voice gave out.
Walking was the only recourse.

Fine Print

According to you,
I made a deal
to be loved and unloved
on repeat.

According to you,
it wouldn't be too much
to dance with death.
A lambada I struggled to perform.

According to you,
I knew and accepted my terms of life,
but then you also knew.

I'm not loved.
Not then.
Not now.
You don't know how.

Father, You Were the Real Grinch,

Before I became a mother,
I thought I was defective.
A return in a crumpled-up package,
stapled closed,
discounted for a quick sale.
Now I know your heart never grew.

I Saw the Signs

Love isn't safe
because you're up ahead
waiting to remind me
of all the reasons
I should hate myself instead.

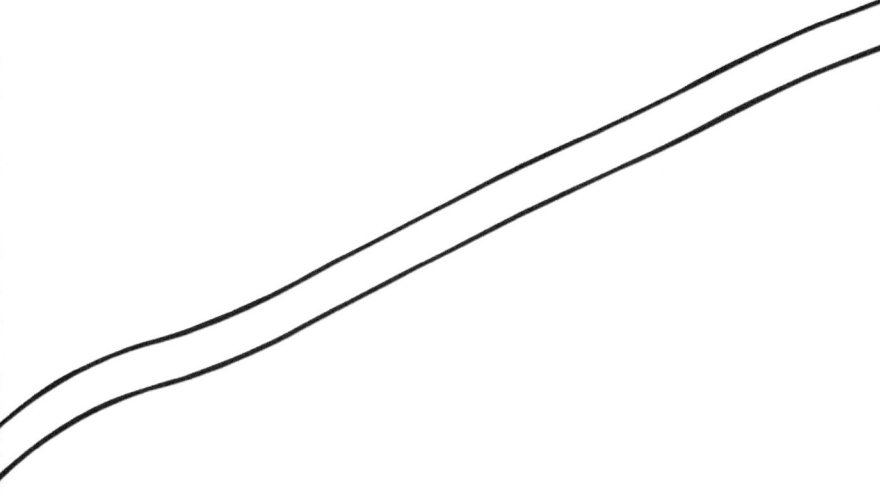

Terms That Should Go Away

Gotcha Day
adoptees aren't dogs.

Tummy Mummy
women are more than incubators.

Can You Be Nostalgic for Moments That Never Happened?

I'm nostalgic
for a life
I never lived
because it's easier
to make believe
than to sit with this pain.

Unsent Letters

Dad,

When you died,
I grieved for the love
I would never have.

Mom,

You might not understand why I walked.
Know this—I never stopped loving you.
I just wish you could've loved yourself
more than the idea of him.

P.S. We deserved better.

Ex-Lover,

You're a wrinkle
I'm glad I ironed out.

Twenty-Year-Old-Me,

You deserved better.

.

P.S. I found better.

I. Ungrateful Adoptee

I won't thank you
for making me stronger.
(I did that on my own.)
You don't get to be
a silver lining
to the trauma you caused.

II. Ungrateful Adoptee

I'm not grateful
for a life I had no choice in.
I'm not grateful
for lessons that wrecked me.
I'm not grateful
for moments that stole my voice.

Don't ask me to be grateful.
I'm hurting; hold my hand instead.

Magic Eight Ball

Stop believing he loves you
when all signs point to:
he loves you not.

Things We Wish the Kept Would Stop Saying

You're lucky.
(We lost our whole damn family.)
DNA doesn't matter
(until it does).
You're a gift.
(We are not commodities.)
You were chosen
(to bear a lifetime of grief).
Adoption is loving.
(All adoptions start with loss.)

Love Me Like a Girl

Calling me your son wasn't a compliment.
It was a reminder being your daughter
wasn't good enough.

Sweet Death

When my people pleaser died,
you begged,

"Bring her back.
I'll do anything."

Except be kind.

Breakup

If karma was my friend,
I would tell her I grew up in chaos.
Chaos feels good
for a minute, but
it's no way to live.
I would ask her:
bring on the boring,
bring on the restful nights,
let me catch my breath.
I would show her
my love language is shifting.
She can't stay.
Loving myself
is all the drama I need.

The Mirror I Didn't Know I Needed

Mirror, mirror,
friend of mine:
reflect my words
back to me.
Break me from this spell.
Show me the good inside of me.

Let Me Be Feral

To be feral
is to speak my mind,
causing flare ups
on a pancake afternoon.
But that would require
embracing the real me,
and she's still tucked
inside the lining of my stomach.
She's still begging to be accepted
by a family that doesn't know
how to love a lost girl.

False Belief

I grew up believing
suicide is a sin
and we are never given
more than we can handle.
I now know
that's not how life works.
The world keeps grinding,
grinding you down to nothing
if you aren't careful.
The best of me
was locked beneath despair.
Despair didn't make me a sinner.
I just needed a hand
to find me again.

Facing Reality

I struggle with labels—
adoptee,
foster care kid—
because I don't want to be those things.

Labels are loss and grief
and struggles and
thoughts of ending it all.

Labels are therapy bills
and disconnection
from myself and others,
with a lifetime subscription
to being misunderstood.

I'm a human first,
with a history I'll never shake,
as though my labels are wired
to my DNA.

I'll always be a lost child,
searching for familiar faces
in a crowd.

That is my reality.

Rinse and Repeat

"What if I spend
the rest of my life chasing love,
only to find her cowering
in the pit of my stomach?

What then?"

"What if you spend
the rest of your life chasing love,
only to find her cowering
in the pit of your stomach?

What then?"

"What if we spend
the rest of our lives chasing love
Only to find her cowering
in the pit of our stomachs?

What then?"

I. Forgiving an Abuser

We talk about forgiveness
like we owe them peace.
Like they haven't already taken
their share and then some.
Like the only way to heal
is to help them heal too.

I don't believe in forgiveness
for people who won't change.

II. Forgiving an Abuser

Forgiveness is bullshit
and their talk is cheap.
We can repair our broken pieces
without also carrying their load.

III. Forgiving an Abuser
(I Forgave Myself Instead)

I haven't named you.
You can rest easy now.
Although I know,
and you know,
and God knows.
Karma may never come.
Justice may never come.
Forgiveness will never come.
She's already here
holding my hand.

The Girl Who Lives

On bad days,
your scripts roll through me
like a bad horror film.
I'm the clumsy girl, stumbling
through your minefield,
trying to stay intact.

Slowly, I'm replacing
the wiring you gave me.
Your stories will not live within me.
I'll be the girl who lives.
I'll be the girl who thrives
at the end of your tale.

I know this because
I kissed the sun
and tucked the moon into bed.

I know this because
my daughter finds
comfort in her momma's arms.

Repeat After Me

You are loved,
so fucking loved.
Say it on repeat,
until you believe it.

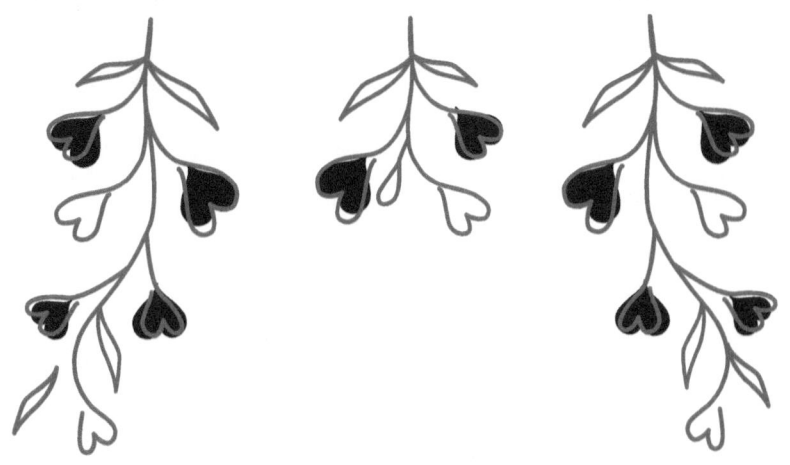

BIG Love

♡ ♡

Loving Ourselves

We should become
our own source of love.
Loving every part,
every imperfection.
Loving the weird,
the wonderful,
the unique.
Basking in all our being.

We should weave love
into every fall and rise,
so when the sun sets,
we know love.
She's our guiding light.

Circle of Insecurity

My husbands says
her and I
are two sharks
circling each other.

The same fish,
salty and fierce,
different oceans.
We're convinced
the other's love
is nothing but a
sandy ambush.

But it's lonely down here
in the depths of the unknown;
it's murky up there
in the land of hope and light.

We keep on circling,
sharing space,
closing the gap.

I'm not sure
we know how to stop,
be at peace
with our rhythms.

Maybe one day stillness
will be our ending
and we can begin.

Same fish, salty and fierce.
Same ocean, healed.

Always and Forever

Brother, I will always love you,
despite the girl who hid in closets,
despite the drugs and cruelty,
despite the damaged walls,
despite all the girls with broken hearts,
despite knowing I'll never understand.
You were not these things to me.

Sent Letters

Love,

What a privilege it is
to have your love.

Mini Love,

You are loved,
so fucking loved.
I'll keep showing you
until my last day,
so that even in death
you'll know my love.

Courting Days

When I was young,
I wanted to be in love,
desperately counting the days
to the next anniversary—
a week, a month, a year.
Trapped in a dynamic
that only experience could untangle.
Then there was you.
Time collapsed.
Ticking dates died alongside the girl
searching to belong,
finding solace in a man
whose love is more than whispered words
in hopes of a steamy night.

Before Marriage

My auntie didn't believe in sex
before marriage.

My brother joked, "She'll die a virgin."

I've laid with men who didn't love me.
Her fate doesn't seem so bad.

The Right Conditions for Love

Connecting with you is different.
You're a friend without an agenda.
A partner who doesn't keep score.

It turns out I'm capable of love,
despite all the assholes
who told me otherwise.
I just needed time
to feel safe.

Work in Progress

I wish saying I love you was easy,
that the words could fall out instead of in.
My relationship with love
is chaotic and complicated.
I can't always trust what I'm feeling.

Love can be painful, like being pinched
and unsafe, like walking down a dark alley.
You're neither scary nor hurtful.
You're joy and sunlight and safety.

Still, I love you is lodged like sludge
around my heart.
I wish I could unclog
my distorted thoughts.
Until then, love me anyways.

What If We Are Meant for More?

We have plans.
All I want to do is stay home
and drift off to anywhere but here.

Maybe I don't deserve fun
for all my selfishness,
pushing for things
I thought we both wanted.
Asking us to be better,
to let go of what ifs
casting us into shadows.

Shadows can't hold my hand,
or call me mommy,
or love me despite a one-track mind.

What ifs
can't change the future,
or take away the pain,
or piece us back together.
Healing is up to you and me.

What if our shadows
lead us to something great?

What then?

Can we step into the light,
accept joy isn't always fleeting
but what we make of it?

Can we be happy,
you and me?

Friends With a Potato

I'd rather share my demons
in between breaths
when there is no time to analyze,
no space to fall apart.
That will come later
when even walking hurts
and I'm too damn tired
to control my thoughts.

But when my past seeps through,
dripping to the floor
in that gap where dark jokes become real
and hurts are no longer secrets,
you see me.
I want my stories back,
devour them,
erase them,
reach into the ether and snatch them up.
But I'm too damn spent
to put up a fight.

So here I am—
healing,
hating you for it.

Sometimes Castles Fall Down

I'm not Rapunzel in a tower,
waiting, watching,
hoping to be rescued.
You're not the Prince,
begging me to run away.

You're the boy with love in his heart
and a brain to match.
I'm the girl building castles in my head,
so high and thick
they blot out the view.

We're not a fairytale.
Sometimes castles fall down.
Stone by stone,
crumbling with the weight of our love,
clearing a path to us.

Picking Sides

I'm always on your side,
even when you can't see it,
even when I don't say it,
even when you push me away,
even when I push back harder,
even when you make me celebrate,
even when I decline dates,
even when you can't hear it,
even when I can't stop the ringing,
even when you'd rather be held then pleased,
even when I don't understand,
even when your POV is skewed,
even when I'm silent.
I draw us a map.
You hand me a compass
because you're always on my side too.

Farewell Scared Girl

Sometimes a sniffle is a sniffle,
not me hiding from you
like a beaten dog.
I'm no longer her—
scared to lean,
or shake you awake,
or call or text,
or snuggle into your chest.
I can ask for comfort
(and vice versa).
Your gift to me.

Space for Children

When we have kids they'll know us—
the real us
with wrinkles and imperfections.
They'll see us laugh.
They'll see us cry.
They'll see it all
and know it's okay to feel it too.
When we hold them
they'll know joy and security,
touch that takes pain away,
words that console.
Their souls will never be too much—
filling spaces with non-stop chatter,
random facts, and stories so wild
we expand to hold them.
In this place,
we'll know and they'll know—love.

Refillable Cup

I've never been good
at loving fully,
leaving enough in reserve
just in case.

But there is something
about our daughter's joy,
a reminder
I'll never run dry.

And if I find myself on empty,
her father is always nearby,
bringing our love
back to me.

You Love Me or You Don't

Love has been all shades of grey except with you.

Heart Murmur

Sometimes I wake
with a heavy chest;
Blue is purring,
mending my heart.

The Lovable Girl

Maybe I'll Start Living

My bedroom door is peppered
with sticky notes,
instructions for a better me.

One by one
they litter my bedroom floor
like fall leaves
shedding in summer.

Some stick to my shoe.
I carry their words,
as I stumble through my day.
Others collect dirt,
slide under my bed,
play on repeat,
invade my dreams.

I can't bring myself to
throw them away.
What will I do
without instructions
for a better me?

To Love Me Is to Listen
(Disenfranchised Grief)

If I tell you adoption is sad,
will you call me names—
unhinged, unhealed, ungrateful?

Will you demand proof
(only to reject my story)?
Will you rage
(what about the abused kids)?
Will you quip back
(I knew a girl; she was loved)
like I'm incapable of more than one emotion?
Or can you sit with my words
without starting a war?

I'm begging you to understand.
I lost:
my mother,
my father,
my siblings,
my history,
my heritage,
my name.

One day here;
the next day gone
like a freak accident
you didn't see coming.

I keep on losing
every time you show me
my feelings aren't valid.

Portrait

I didn't go looking for love.
She found me
as I searched her face
in a vintage photo of me,
wondering how the
have-it-all girl
lost her way.

She disappeared in a mirage
of shoulds.
Shrinking to the size of a thumbtack,
she pricked my throat
as she slid into a hollow of snakes.

There she waited
to regain her strength.
She clawed her way back out,
leaving my cords open and bruised.
Ready to be loved again.

Say It Louder for the Girl in the Back

If I keep telling myself
I'm loved,
I'm so fucking loved,
maybe I'll start believing it.

I Will Not Pass Down This Pain
(Thoughts On Therapy)

If I don't change
what was the point
of cutting myself open
week after week?

You're the reason (little girl).
I'm the reason (hurt child).
We are the reason (momma and daughter)
I'll keep on healing.
Failure will destroy us both.

Cycle Breaker

Mornings arrive early
before the hum of birds
and worker bee traffic.
Wisps of sleep cling to me,
as I greet my mini love.
Her smile is stomach deep—
happiness before hunger.
I hunger for her joy,
filling up on her need to be held.
Coos and trills,
an everlasting feast.
I know she'll thrive
in ways I struggled to.

Antidote

When you encounter cruelty,
seek kindness.
Counteract their hurt.
Draw out their poison
in the presence of love.
Do not continue to consume their pain
in hopes of becoming immune.
It will not work
to lift the heavy from your chest.
Be in nature.
Laugh with a friend.
Sleep in.
Listen to music.
Soak up all the good
the world has to offer.

This is your antidote—
to ~~survive~~ thrive
in what can be a cruel world.

We Won't Always Feel So Sad

On days of sadness
I've been teaching myself
to text, *I love you.*
A jolt to my heart
to keep on breathing.
A reminder
feeling is the path to healing.
If I can feel the sad now
then I can feel joy again.

And so can you.

Healed Girl Summer

Once upon a time,
I wished I could hibernate,
get full on life,
then slip away until the warmth returns.
I'd trust the world wouldn't disturb me.
I'd trust I'm safe, and worthy of rest—
a pie-in-the-sky dream
not meant for losers like me.

Now, I take comfort in slumbering trees,
beautifully wrapped in a cover of snow.
Underneath tangled roots,
magical worlds unfold
while above, the night sky dances.
Anything is possible,
like shedding old stories in time for summer.

II. Someone Worthy of Love

~~Me~~
~~Me~~
~~Me~~
~~Me~~
~~Me~~
~~Me~~
~~Me~~
~~Me~~
~~ME~~
~~ME~~
~~ME~~
~~ME~~
~~ME~~
~~ME~~

ME!
FINALLY ME!

Love & War

I couldn't love the girl
you only seemed to despise.
I chose to love me instead,
withdrawing from a war
I was never going to win.

The Price of Happiness

If you had asked me years ago
what I thought of my family,
I would've sworn they were the best.
Anything to keep myself from losing them.

But in the end, I lost them anyway,
because sometimes scapegoats
jump the fence
and realize the grass is greener
on the other side.

Scapegoat

I'm told I'm the reason
unkind words
swirl around me.
They reach inside my head,
persuading me I'm not enough
and I'm at fault.

I'm told the old me
must resurrect,
lie down,
grin and bear it.
Be a peach, sweet and soft,
ripe for the taking.

I'm told to move forward
I must move back,
choke on their ugly words,
accept their choices as my own.
Their tears
twist my shame deeper,
silencing my growth,
binding me to untruths.

I'm told
I'm nothing without them.
I'm stupid enough
to engage in a fight
I can't win.
I'm a moving target
that will never be enough.

I'm told
if I try harder,
be nice,
be quiet,
be perfect,
then everything will go back to normal.

But I will not hold
secrets that do me harm.

I will not tread softly on thin ice.
I'm already drowning,
trapped in a persona
they want me to be.
A dumping ground for hostility.

I will not take responsibility
for others' actions.

ALMOST LOVED

I will not accept degradation
for the benefit of egos.

I will not apologize
for people afraid of their shadows.

I've been in the dark.
My demons have made me fierce
when I was brave enough
to do battle,
to be better,
to surround myself with love,
replace all the ugly words.

I'm worthy of love
despite groupthink,
even when they can't see it,
even if they don't believe it.
They no longer get space
when they bring darkness.

It's taken a hell of a long time
to realize
I'm no longer willing
to be a scapegoat.

Certified Copy

I'm no longer
the broken thing,
you tried so hard to break.
I'm love, and light, and laughter.
I'm the rainbow after the storm.
I'm the swirl of light dancing in the night.
I'm a vibrant red,
embracing the girl
I should've been from the start.

Love Hits Differently

I've been called hateful things,
but never from those who love me.

Friend in Arms

Take my story if it makes you brave.
Take my voice until yours returns.
Take my eyes to see yourself
(wonderfully unique).
Take my knowing
so that one day you'll know too
(you're deeply loved).
Take it all; step up beside me.

Love + Adoption

Love
isn't enough

Love + Adoptee

Love
we were always worthy.

Open Letter to Adopters

Stop sharing our stories.
Stop centering your feelings over ours.
Stop gatekeeping our information.
Stop expecting gratitude.
Stop villainizing our first families.
Please stop, because we deserve a safe space.
We deserve to be loved.

Sincerely,
an adoptee

Becoming the Lovable Girl

Love doesn't come with strings.
I'll cut every cord
if you can't love me for me.

Lifeline

I tell my dog I love her
and with her, life is brighter.
She snuggles into my side,
sighing out the day.
A reminder,
she sees me the same way.

Tell Your Friends You Love Them

I don't tell my friends I love them
but with you it was almost too late,
so I'll say it now.

I love you because you're safe
and understand friendship
has seasons and moods and trials.
We can disappear for a minute
and reappear and pick up again.

I love you because you listen
and understand being a mirror
is being a good friend.

I'm sorry it took a near death
and you saying it first.
So my dear friend, hear me now:
I love you. I love you. I love you.

A Lesson in the Making

There are times
I feel unloved,
but I know
I'm not unlovable.

Infinite

When the stars shine,
my soul pushes against my ribcage
to notice the vastness,
the wonder, that kid me had
sitting on top of grandma's shed.
Where nothing was out of reach.

Skeleton Guest

I had dinner with a skeleton.
The bones of past and present
picked apart,
nick by nick.
We held each other
and became a mirror to all
that has been lost, gained,
rediscovered.

I had dinner with a skeleton,
then I kicked his ass out
in time to greet tomorrow.
My past no longer rattles me.

Stockholm Syndrome

Your truth held me captive.
I wished to be a version
you could love.

There were no actions
(short of an identity change)
that could've made that happen.

Truth—you didn't deserve me.

Zeus Can Go to Hades

Sometimes I want to be feral
without explaining,
sneaking off to cry,
blocking my love from witnessing
the tsunami inside me.
There are no shortcuts
to feeling my way through,
wave after wave,
with promise of reprieve,
or at least an abandoned beach.
Salty and fierce,
I become Aphrodite,
reclaiming stolen goods,
rising from a sea of wreckage,
no longer willing to shiver
in Zeus' presence.

When Rage Covers Sadness

Rage may be a secondary feeling.
Still, you warm my chest,
radiate through me,
steady and quiet
as we move towards a new comfort.

I accept the parts of me
that kept me company,
that let me live.
But I'm in my season of healing,
so my neon love,
I kiss you goodnight.

Fire Walk

Hope doesn't mean
I'm done sifting through ashes
of burned bridges and distorted images,
leaving footprints in that gap
between thriving and surviving.

Hope doesn't mean I'm okay,
only that I'm healing.
One day I'll be ready
to scatter these ashes.

When Flowers Die Remember

When flowers die
they haunt the mantel
of my childhood home.

They are pressed between pages,
stamps of sunnier days.

They are scattered on our wedding table,
fragrant reminders I'm wanted.

Now that our love has aged,
when flowers die
I don't hold them hostage
in glass vases—
no longer afraid
love will leave me.

Let Me Count the Ways

I'm loved by a man who stands with me.
By our mini love who breathes joy.
By friends who understand.
By me, *finally*,
at least for today.

Guess What?

I miss you.
The old you.
The roll-over-and-take-it you—
the shut up, closed up, garbage heap.

I miss you.
The hollow you.
The always-smiling you—
my dumping ground of inadequacies.

I miss you.
The polite you.
The give-but-never-take you—
the sidelined, flat-lined, voiceless dump.

I miss you.
The stupid you.
The do-as-you're-told-you.

Guess what?
That *bitch* is dead!

When Love Shows

Today will be a slow morning,
honouring my body's need for rest.
Because I've finally learned
to love myself first.

Family Puzzle

I may never be whole,
bits of me hidden in a child's pocket
like I'm a Christmas Eve puzzle.
The family searches for the stolen piece.

I may never be whole,
but I will never be a second-hand puzzle,
good enough for a discounted price.

I no longer accept
her hand-me-down tales.
I'm not a give-away in a tarnished box.

She's worthy.
I'm worthy.
To claim the lost piece.

You are loved.

Author's Note

Adoption is amazing.
Adoption is brave.
Adoption is (insert happy story).

Beneath the surface of every adoption story is a hurt child who lost everything. Even when outside care is needed, every adoption starts with loss.

Adoptee grief is widely misunderstood. We aren't given space to feel our feelings. While adoption is often exciting for a new parent, it's complicated for an adoptee. Our feelings are overshadowed by the centering of others' feelings of joy. This is what disenfranchised grief is. This is how the world shows us we don't matter. The game of pretending begins. We become lost in a fog of gratitude and servitude. Some of us never make it out.

Thank you for reading my collection. Your act of picking up my book makes me feel less alone and I hope my poems have done the same for you.

You are worthy.

Adoptees,

We keep so much inside. Too much inside. It's okay to feel however you feel. Feeling the loss of your first family doesn't make you ungrateful. Wanting to connect with your first family doesn't make you disloyal. Loving your adoptive family doesn't mean you don't need answers.

Wherever you are in your journey, I'm sending you love and understanding. Your voice matters.

XO

Rena

You are enough.

Acknowledgments

Thank you to my fellow adoptees for helping me find my voice.

Thank you to Shelby Leigh for her keen editorial eye and her gentle and encouraging style. You truly made this book better.

Thank you to my readers for supporting my work and helping me feel less alone.

Thank you to the poetry community for making me believe I could, in fact, publish a poetry collection.

Thank you to my potato friend for reminding me anxiety is a bitch and imposter syndrome can fuck right off. This world is brighter with you in it.

Thank you to my loves for loving me.

Thank you to me for writing this book and continuing to do the work to heal.

If you enjoyed this book, please subscribe to my newsletter at TheJoyConnection.substack.com and consider leaving a review on Amazon and Goodreads. I'd so appreciate any kind words you have to share. Thank you so much for reading.

About the Author

Rena Joy comes from Halifax, Nova Scotia. She now lives in rural Alberta, where she dreams of oceans and one day returning to her birthplace. Poetry is her first love. She found poetry at the age of eleven, following the sudden death of her brother. Poetry has become a safe space to process her emotions. Rena now uses poetry to build connections, heal and break stigmas.

Almost Loved is her debut collection of poems, inspired by her own life and the beautiful humans that have helped her heal and grow. Rena's hope is to offer readers a place to feel heard and space to embrace their lovable selves.

Outside of writing, Rena loves exploring the outdoors with her little and her bulldog, Queenie.

For more poetry
Instagram @renajoypoetry
TikTok @renajoypoetry
www.renajoypoetry.com

www.ingramcontent.com/pod-product-compliance
Lightning Source LLC
Chambersburg PA
CBHW030437010526
44118CB00011B/684